Mountain Sports

Andrew Luke

MASON CREST

Adventurous Outdoor Sports Series

Air Sports

All-Terrain Sports

Mountain Sports

Snow Sports

Water Sports

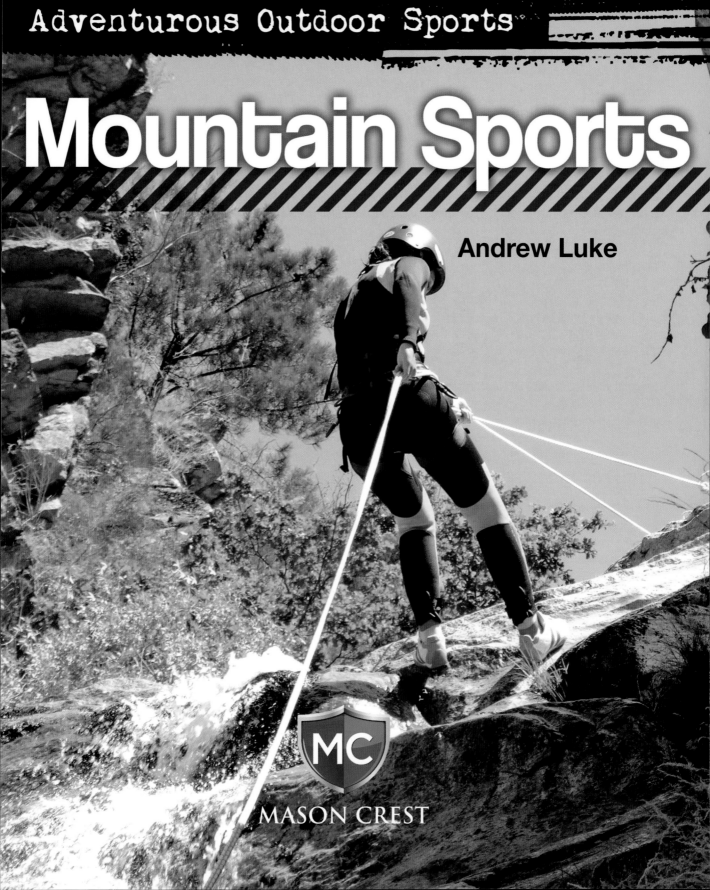

Mountain Sports

Andrew Luke

MASON CREST

MASON CREST
450 Parkway Drive, Suite D
Broomall, Pennsylvania 19008
(866) MCP-BOOK (toll-free)

Andrew Luke

First printing
9 8 7 6 5 4 3 2 1

ISBN (hardback) 978-1-4222-3707-6
ISBN (series) 978-1-4222-3704-5
ISBN (ebook) 978-1-4222-8080-5

Cover and Interior designed by Tara Raymo; www.creativelytara.com

Cataloging-in-Publication Data on file with the Library of Congress

QR CODES AND LINKS TO THIRD-PARTY CONTENT
You may gain access to certain third-party content ("Third-Party Sites") by scanning and using the QR Codes that appear in this publication (the "QR Codes"). We do not operate or control in any respect any information, products, or services on such Third-Party Sites linked to by us via the QR Codes included in this publication, and we assume no responsibility for any materials you may access using the QR Codes. Your use of the QR Codes may be subject to terms, limitations or restrictions set forth in the applicable terms of use or otherwise established by the owners of the Third-Party Sites. Our linking to such Third-Party Sites via the QR Codes does not imply an endorsement or sponsorship of such Third-Party Sites, or the information, products, or services offered on or through the Third- Party Sites, nor does it imply an endorsement or sponsorship of this publication by the owners of such Third-Party Sites.

Table of Contents

Key icons to look for:

Words to Understand: These words with their easy-to-understand definitions will increase the reader's understanding of the text while building vocabulary skills.

Text-Dependent Questions: These questions send the reader back to the text for more careful attention to the evidence presented there.

Sidebars: This boxed material within the main text allows readers to build knowledge, gain insights, explore possibilities, and broaden their perspectives by weaving together additional information to provide realistic and holistic perspectives.

Research Projects: Readers are pointed toward areas of further inquiry connected to each chapter. Suggestions are provided for projects that encourage deeper research and analysis.

Educational Videos: Readers can view videos by scanning our QR codes, providing them with additional educational content to supplement the text. Examples include news coverage, moments in history, speeches, iconic sports moments and much more!

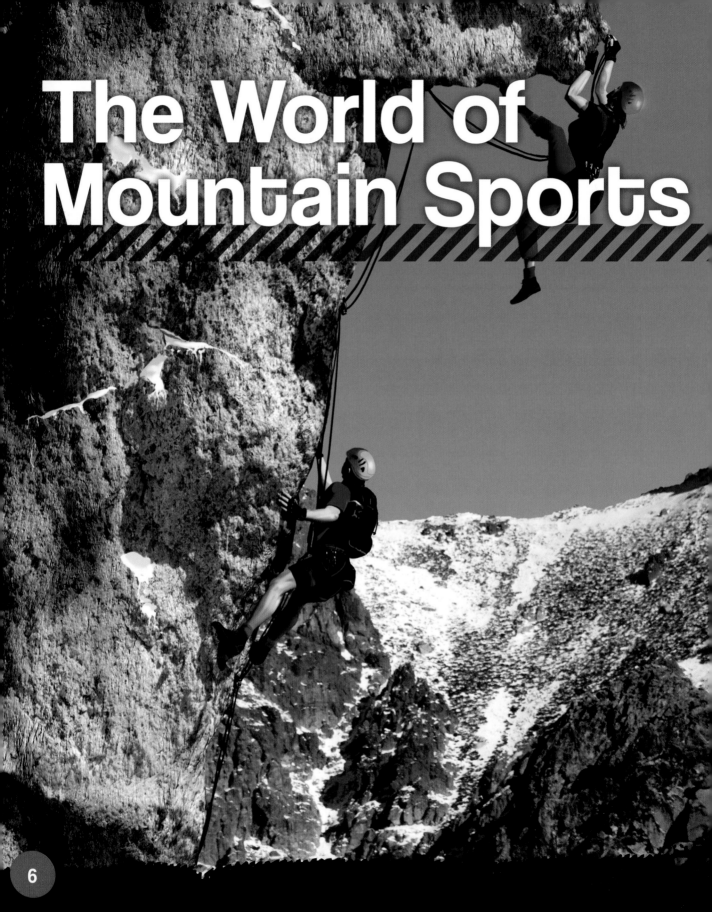

The World of Mountain Sports

For some people, the mountains have always called to them. When vacation time rolls around, they head inland rather than to the shore. A dense forest that climbs over rough terrain satisfies them more than any stretch of white sand ever could.

There is a certain segment of the mountain-loving population who seek more than hiking and nature walks have to offer. They are looking to be challenged by their mountains, whether it be traversing a canyon, climbing a towering peak, or scaling a sheer rock face with their bare hands; adventure seekers and adrenaline junkies find plenty of satisfaction high above sea level.

Of course, the natural competitiveness of humans has manifested itself in our mountainous pursuits. It was never going to be enough to just do these things. The question had to be satisfied as to who could do them fastest, best, or most often.

Competitions, both organized and not, have sprung up around just about every mountain sport. How many mountains have you climbed (and how high were they)? How long did it take you to figure out how to get to the top of that massive boulder? Can you climb up that cliff, and can you do it without the help of ropes? Or, how about with no equipment at all? How long does it take you to run 40 km (25 miles) straight uphill?

These are the questions that men and women now compete to answer in the varied world of mountain sports.

Free Climbing

Free climbers scale the sides of mountains using only their own strength, stamina, and balance to help them climb.

 ## Words to Understand

etiquette: proprieties of conduct as established in any class or community or for any occasion.

honed: made more acute or effective.

innovate: to introduce something new; make changes in anything established.

True free climbers will tackle a route on sight, meaning without inspecting it first.

Free climbing is not referring to a lucky instance where a climber does not have to pay. Instead, it means that the climber has chosen to employ a climbing technique that is free from any assistance in making upward progress. Generally, to qualify as a free climb, climbers cannot use their equipment to help them. Although they can use rope to prevent a fall, if climbers use a rope to support body weight other than in the event of a fall, it is no longer free climbing.

Traditional free climbers take the concept of free climbing quite seriously. This includes certain climbing **etiquette** that upholds the integrity of a free climb. For example, it is considered bad form to inspect the climbing route before attempting it. True free climbers will make the attempt "on sight," meaning the first time they see the route is the first time they attempt to climb it.

Free climbers are also a creative bunch. Major respect is given to those climbers who **innovate** new routes up established ascents or take fresh approaches to well-established routes.

Today's free climber generation has **honed** their craft in climbing gyms, which came to prominence around the world in the 1990s. Climbing gyms allow climbers to train on routes with different grades, or levels of difficulty, at the same convenient location, unlike traditional outdoor rock climbers, who may have to travel several thousand miles (or kilometers) to find climbs of significantly tougher grades.

Unlike those who go to climbing gyms, traditional outdoor free climbers have to travel to find locations that offer them varying difficulty levels.

Sidebar

Free climbing has a grading system that denotes the difficulty of climbing a given route. The system was developed in the 1950s by the Sierra Club and is known as the Yosemite Decimal Rating System (YRDS). The YRDS breaks climbing routes down by class and then by grade.

Class 1: This involves walking on an established trail.

Class 2: Here, climbers hike up a steep incline.

Class 3: This is climbing up a steep hillside with solid footing; hands and feet are necessary.

Class 4: This is exposed climbing. A rope would be used to belay past places where a fall could be lethal.

Class 5: This is where vertical rock climbing begins. A three-point stance (two hands and a foot or two feet and a hand) is needed at all times. The person leading needs a rope and protection as an unprotected fall from a Class 5 climb would be harmful if not fatal. Class 5 climbs are subdivided into grades to give more detail.

Class 5.0-5.6: These are your starter grades for beginners to vertical climbing. Becoming trickier as you progress up the grade scale, most of these routes will still have multiple hand- and footholds for every move.

Class 5.7-5.10: This is expert territory, so only experienced climbers should attempt these routes. A 5.7 will take patience and skill, whereas a 5.10 will take those things plus strength, endurance, and serious skills.

Class 5.11-5.14: These are dangerous routes, even for experts. Hand- and footholds are rare. Free climbing is next to impossible.

Text-Dependent Questions

1. What does the term *free climbing* mean?
2. What does it mean when a climber attempts a route "on sight"?
3. When did climbing gyms come to prominence?

Research Project

Investigate the types of graded climbs that are close to where you live. What is the highest class of routes within 100 miles (161 km) of your house? How far is the closest Class 5 route? If there is more than one Class 5 route, what is the highest grade of all of them?

One piece of aid that free climbers do allow themselves is chalk, which improves grip by keeping hands dry.

Educational Video

Scan here to watch a free climbing video.

Aid Climbing

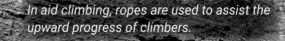
In aid climbing, ropes are used to assist the upward progress of climbers.

Words to Understand

belay: to secure by attaching to a person or to an object offering stable support.

étriers: a short, portable ladder or set of webbing loops that can be attached to a karabiner.

karabiners: D-shaped rings with a spring catch on one side, used for fastening ropes in mountaineering.

Sometimes even the best climbers come across a problem they just cannot solve with their own two hands. In these situations, assistance is needed, which is where we get the term *aid climbing*. As opposed to free climbing, in aid climbing equipment is used to actually help climbers make upward progress, not just to stop a fall.

When a challenging section presents itself on an ascent, such as a steep outcropping or long sections that require more strength or endurance than the climber possesses, aid climbing is the best option. Typically, climbers use anchored **karabiners** with **étriers** or stirrups and a two-person system with one climber on lead and the other on **belay**. This allows the lead climber, standing in the stirrups while attached to his or her partner, to reach up to areas where there are better holds to continue a free climb or to insert another anchor that allows the aided climb to continue.

Aid climbing is much slower and more cumbersome than free climbing,

Aid climbing is slower and more cumbersome than free climbing.

as it requires hauling a large amount of gear and time to set the equipment. Where it once was the standard, aid climbing has also fallen out of favor with modern climbers as the standard equipment (permanent, penetrating anchors like pitons) tends to damage the natural holds in the rock face. More recently, however, aid equipment has been developed that, rather than being fixed like pitons, are removable. Use of this type of equipment is known as clean aid.

In a typical two-person climbing team scenario, one climber is on lead, and the second is on belay.

Sidebar

Like free climbing, aid climbing has a grading system of its own:
- A0 - This climb requires only the occasional aid maneuver.
- A1 - A beginner-level climb in which the climber uses straightforward aid placements and some aid climbing gear.
- A2-A3 - These are intermediate-level grades for routes that will include a few complicated placements and specific aid gear but have no real fall danger.
- A3+-A4 - These are advanced-level routes where the climbing is difficult, even with aid, as placements are consistently complicated and the chances of a long fall are substantial.
- A5 - This indicates an extremely technical, expert-level climb with the potential for deadly falls.

Text-Dependent Questions

1. What does aid climbing equipment help climbers do?
2. What are the climbers in a two-person aid system called?
3. What is the use of removable aid equipment called?

Research Project

Do some research on the move away from fixed aid climbing to clean aid climbing. Document the timeline from when fixed aid was the norm through the shift in ideas that made clean aid the preferred method.

Karabiners like this are often part of the equipment used by aid climbers.

Educational Video

Scan here to see a video that shows you how people aid climb.

Bouldering

Indoor bouldering competitions take place in climbing gyms and feature walls up to 30 feet (9 m) high.

Words to Understand

artistry: artistic ability or skill.

dynamic: always active or changing.

pitch: degree of slope.

Bouldering is the mountain sport that combines an aspect of **artistry** with the sport element of climbing. In bouldering, climbers use no rope to assist them as they attempt to free climb rock formations that are typically about 20 feet (6 m) high but can range up to 30 feet (9 m).

Bouldering is not simply about climbing. The art of the sport comes from the problem solving required to succeed at it. Originating in France in the early 1900s, the problem-solving element was added mid-century by American John Gill, known in the sport as the father of modern bouldering. Gill described bouldering as "one **pitch** climbing of great difficulty, done close to the ground and un-roped with some kind of **dynamic** component."

Gill scored that dynamic component with his B1, B2, B3 system. Climbers start at a designated spot at the bottom of the boulder and have to overcome challenges in the route to the top, with B1 being the easiest climbs and B3 the toughest. Those challenges used to be naturally occurring in the rock surfaces, such as cracks in granite or overhangs in sandstone. In the modern version of the sport, competitions often take place indoors on man-made climbing walls.

The International Federation of Sports Climbing (IFSC), the Italy-based governing body for competitive climbing, sanctions bouldering competitions. This includes the IFSC Climbing World Championships, which are held every other year.

Colored holds mark the route climbers must navigate to score points.

In bouldering, climbers use no safety equipment such as ropes or harnesses.

Sidebar

Since 2007, the IFSC has held the Climbing World Cup. The IFSC took over the event from the Union Internationale des Associations d'Alpinisme (UIAA, or International Climbing and Mountaineering Federation in English). The France-based UIAA, which is the international governing body of climbing and mountaineering, focuses on equipment safety, grading climbing routes, and setting training standards. Therefore although the UIAA held the first World Cup season in 1989, it made sense to transfer it to the sport climbing-focused IFSC.

The World Cup is a season-long series of competitions held at venues across the globe in three categories: bouldering, lead, and speed. Austria's Anna Stöhr is one of the top boulderers in the world. She won three consecutive World Cup titles in bouldering from 2011 to 2013 to go along with her 2008 title and two IFSC World Championships.

On the men's side, Adam Ondra of the Czech Republic is one of the top climbers in the world. He was the IFSC World Cup overall winner (most points in all three categories) in 2009 at just 16 years old. The following year he won both the bouldering and overall World Cup titles. In 2014, Ondra was the IFSC bouldering world champion.

Text-Dependent Questions

1. What is the typical height of a bouldering formation?
2. Who is the father of modern bouldering?
3. Where is the IFSC based?

Research Project

Check out a climbing gym near you. Practice bouldering routes and compare the different types of problems different routes present.

Educational Video

Watch a bouldering video by scanning this QR code.

Solo Climbing

Solo climbers face the challenge of the rock face on their own, with no partner nearby to help if they get in trouble.

Words to Understand

engages: moves into position so as to come into operation.

essentially: the basic, fundamental, or intrinsic nature of a person, thing, or situation.

fatal: causing or capable of causing death.

In solo climbing, climbers do not have the assistance of a partner or partners. It is them versus the rock face, trying to find the best route to the top.

This is not to say that solo climbers have no help. In roped soloing, climbers have the choice to either free climb or aid climb. The difference between the two is whether or not the climber puts body weight on the rope. Using the rope to support the body's weight is a form of aid climbing.

If the rope is used only as a safety device that **engages** only in the event of a fall, then it is a free climb. In the IFSC World Cup, Lead is one of the three events (along with Bouldering and Speed) and is essentially a roped free soloing event.

Mina Markovič of Slovenia is one of the best women in the world in the Lead event. In 2011, 2012, and 2015 she

In roped soloing, climbers can use the rope for safety or for aid as well.

was the World Cup season champion in Lead. Markovič was also the overall World Cup champion in three straight years from 2011 to 2013. Her main competitors are Austria's Angela Eiter and South Korea's Kim Jain. Eiter is a four-time world champion in Lead. She has also won three World Cup titles in Lead and the overall World Cup title in 2006. Kim is a three-time World Cup champion in Lead, a two-time overall World Cup champion, and the 2014 IFSC Lead world champion.

Solo climbers can, of course, choose to climb without a rope. This kind of free soloing is one of the most dangerous sports in the world. It is **essentially** extreme bouldering, as instead of 30 feet (9 m), the climbs are several hundred feet (over 30 m). The climber uses no equipment beyond climbing shoes and a helmet, meaning a fall could result in serious or **fatal** injury.

When the rope supports body weight, the climb is considered to be aided.

Sidebar

Californian Alex Honnold is widely considered to be the world's best free soloist. Using only his bare hands and a pair of climbing shoes, he has scaled some of the steepest, most sheer rock faces on the planet, including these:

- Regular NW Face of Half Dome in Yosemite Valley, CA – 2,000 feet (610 m)
- El Sendero Luminoso in Mexico – 1,750 feet (533 m)
- Moonlight Buttress in Utah's Zion National Park – 1,200 feet (366 m)
- University Wall, Squamish, BC, Canada – 900 feet (274 m)

Text-Dependent Questions

1. What kind of event is the Lead on the IFSC World Cup?
2. Name a woman who won three consecutive IFSC overall World Cup titles.
3. Who is the 2014 world champion in women's lead climbing?

Research Project

Find videos of Alex Honnold on the Internet. Which are considered to be his greatest climbs, and why? What sets him apart from other free soloists?

Lead climbing is an example of roped free soloing.

Educational Video

Scan here for an action-packed video on solo climbing.

Ice Climbing

This is what ice climbing at the Perito Moreno Glacier in Patagonia, Argentina, looks like.

Words to Understand

alpine: of, pertaining to, on, or part of any lofty mountain.

protection: anchoring equipment placed in cracks for safety while rock climbing.

scaling: climbing up or over something high and steep.

An ice ax and crampons are essential tools for ice climbing.

There are those in this world for whom the challenge of scaling a Class 5 rock face is not challenging enough. That is simply too comfortable for a certain breed of climber. So these people wait until the weather turns, winter blows in, and vertical surfaces either become covered in ice or turn to ice entirely.

Ice climbers prefer to climb surfaces such as frozen waterfalls, iced-over rock faces, and icefalls. In climbing, ice is generally of two varieties: **alpine** and water.

Alpine ice is the frozen precipitation found near the top of high mountains. Ice climbers do not necessarily seek out this type of ice as a challenge but rather come across it as part of a larger route up a mountain. Alpine ice is considered to be less technical and easier to climb than water ice.

Water ice is once flowing or cascading water that has frozen. Ice climbers seeking a more technical challenge will go looking for a frozen waterfall to scale.

Scaling an icy face using a two-person rope system requires the same equipment and technique as rock climbing. The exception is that ice screws are needed as the **protection** anchors for the rope. The climbing technique that is most unique to ice surfaces is called front pointing. This technique requires the use of ice axes and crampons, which are metal spikes that attach to boots are used for traction. On a vertical surface, the climber kicks into the ice with the crampons to get a foothold and then swings the ax into the ice above to create a hold there. This is repeated up the length of the surface; it's slow going and hard on the calf muscles but very effective.

On lower-graded climbs it is possible to traverse horizontally across steps in the ice to find the best route.

Sidebar

One of the most popular places in the world to ice climb is in the Canadian Rockies, where just as for aid and free climbing, ice climbing has a grading system. The scale runs from WI1 at the least difficult end up to WI7 at the top. From WI1 to WI5+, the vertical climb is segmented with steps every 10 to 20 meters (33 to 66 feet). Protection is generally needed starting at WI4. WI6, WI6+, and WI7-graded climbs are vertical for the entire pitch.

 Text-Dependent Questions

1. Where is alpine ice found?
2. Which presents the more technical challenge for climbers: alpine or water ice?
3. What two pieces of equipment are needed for front pointing?

 **Research Project**

Make a list of the special equipment needed by ice climbers, and compare to the equipment used in traditional rock climbing. What are the biggest differences?

 Educational Video

Scan here to see ice climbing in action.

Canyoneering

Canyons with narrow gorges and multiple drops are the best test of skills such as rappelling and scrambling.

Words to Understand

hydraulics: pressurized liquid generates great force or power.

inherently: belonging to the basic nature of something.

scrambling: walking up steep terrain involving the use of one's hands.

Canyoneering (called canyoning outside of the United States) as an organized adventure sport is relatively new. Its origins as an activity, however, are centuries old. Humans have been exploring canyons around the world throughout history. In North America, evidence exists of the Anasazi people inhabiting the canyon country of Colorado more than 2,000 years ago.

Today, canyoneering is more than just exploring. The term has come to refer to the technical navigation of a canyon using a variety of techniques, such as climbing, **scrambling**, rappelling, and swimming.

The sport has grown in popularity since the late 1990s, and organizations have sprung up to support it over the years. In 1995, the Commission Internationale de Canyon (CIC, or International Canyoning Commission in English) was formed in France. Now headquartered in Germany, the CIC offers canyoneering guide certification that must be renewed every three years to ensure the highest safety standards. In 1999, the American Canyoneering Academy began training canyoneering guides for professional certification.

Training is not required for the sport as anyone can go to a canyon and try to climb down into it. This is, however, **inherently** dangerous, and taking safety and training courses just makes sense. There are techniques and equipment to master and dangerous situations to prepare for.

A climber rappels or abseils down a waterfall.

Rivers carve canyons, and therefore there are water dynamics at play in most canyoneering situations. Water **hydraulics**, undercurrents, and flash floods are just a few examples of dangers that canyoneers must be aware of.

Of course, there are climbing hazards as well as narrow passages with jagged walls that dictate the proper use of helmets, ropes, and other safety equipment.

A canyoneering instructor drills holes in a rock to prepare a route for climbing.

Sidebar

Canyoneering is one of the most gear intensive of all mountain sports. The sport typically presents several different condition or terrain types in a single exploration, so canyoneers need to be prepared for anything. A list of items a canyoneer needs to consider carefully before embarking includes:

Water – Staying hydrated is essential. Experts suggest using an expandable reservoir rather than a plastic bottle to save room in your pack.

Proper clothing – Wool socks, thin nylon jackets with synthetic insulation, permeable shoes with excellent gripping soles, and rubber-coated knit gloves are good choices.

Wetsuit – Canyon water sees little sun, so it will be cold. If your chosen canyon has extended swims, a 4mm wetsuit (and neoprene socks) will be the favorite item you bring.

Climbing gear – You'll need static polyester rope, a rope bag, harness, karabiners, descenders, and black webbing.

Other gear – 35-45 liter (1-1.5 cubic foot) backpack, dry bag, headlamp, helmet, first-aid kit, and sunscreen are crucial.

GPS – Signal strength can be spotty depending on how far off the beaten path you roam, but it's a good idea to have one in your dry bag if needed (in addition to your paper map and a compass)!

Text-Dependent Questions

1. What is canyoneering called outside the United States?
2. When was the CIC formed?
3. Name three dangers that water presents for canyoneers.

Research Project

Where are the best spots for canyoneering near where you live? Pick the top three, and list the features that canyoneering enthusiasts find most appealing about each.

Canyoneers navigate a river in the Aragon region of Spain.

Educational Video

Watch this amazing canyoneering video.

Mountaineering

A group of climbers prepare for dinner at a Mount Everest base camp.

 ## Words to Understand

conquered: to gain victory over, surmount, master, or overcome.

daunting: causing fear or discouragement, intimidating.

noble: of an admirably high quality, notably superior, or excellent.

The quest to stand on the peak of any mountain starts at the bottom, and enormous dedication is required to make the summit.

Mountaineering, or alpinism as it is also known, used to simply refer to the quest to climb to the top of the mountains, to stand on their very peaks. The modern meaning has added various aspects to the term, but it still primarily means mountain climbing.

The first recorded climb, meaning an organized effort of some technical difficulty, was the 1492 ascent of Mont Aguille (2,085 m [6,841 feet]) in France by Antoine de Ville. In the 1700s and early 1800s, many of Europe's great mountains were summited for the first time. By the end of the 19th century, in an era now known as the "golden age of alpinism," mountain climbing was regarded as a **noble** pursuit and was a full-time effort for many adventurers.

By 1913, with the climbing of Alaska's Mount McKinley (now called Denali) by Hudson Stuck, most of the world's highest mountains outside the Himalaya range in Asia had been summited. Many of the tallest Himalayan peaks were **conquered** in the 1950s, including most famously, the world's highest mountain, Mount Everest, in 1953 by Sir Edmund Hillary.

Today, modern mountaineers have two main challenges: the Eight Thousanders and the Seven Summits. The Eight Thousanders is the more **daunting** challenge as it refers to the 14 peaks in the world that are more than 8,000 meters (26,247 feet) above sea level. The challenge is to have climbed to the top of every one.

The Seven Summits challenge involves climbing the highest peak on each of the seven continents: Antarctica, North America, Africa, South America, Europa, Asia, and Australia.

Today's modern climbing gear, including oxygen tanks and gear that is more efficient, lighter, warmer, and stronger, has made these challenges more accessible and has made each climb two to three times faster. Still, an enormous level of commitment is required to join the ranks of the dedicated few to complete both challenges.

At 8,848 meters (29,030 feet) above sea level, the top of Mount Everest is the highest place in the world.

Sidebar

Italy's Reinhold Messner was the first verified member of the Eight Thousander club. He climbed his 14th peak, Lhotse in Nepal, in 1986. The club has 32 other members, the last two of which joined in 2014. Of the 33 members, 15, including Messner, have climbed all 14 peaks without the aid of supplemental oxygen, which is often used in high-altitude mountaineering. Purists of the sport claim that using bottled oxygen is just like cheating in other sports by using steroids or blood doping. Messner is a believer that climbing without oxygen adheres to the highest standard of mountaineering. Supplemental oxygen makes breathing at the top of an Eight Thousander peak feel more like a Four Thousander, which is why many climbers say oxygen "brings the mountain down." It is, however, much safer as an oxygen-starved body can shut down quickly.

Text-Dependent Questions

1. Who was the first person to lead an expedition to the summit of Mount McKinley?
2. How many mountains in the world are higher than 8,000 meters (26,247 feet)?
3. What is the Seven Summits challenge?

Research Project

Investigate the Seven Summits challenge, and outline the difference between the Messner version and the Bass version. Which version do you agree with, and why?

Educational Video

Scan here to watch a video on mountaineering.

Skyrunning

Skyrunners practice their craft by running for hours in oxygen-depleted mountain air.

 Words to Understand

incline: a slanting surface.

ridge: the place where two sloping surfaces meet.

sanctions: to give effective or authoritative approval or consent to.

Runners challenge themselves by running increasingly greater distances, such as the 5 km (3 mile), the 10 km (6 mile), the half marathon, the full marathon, and all the way up to 100-km (62 mile) ultramarathon. The sport of skyrunning is different. Rather than challenging runners to run farther, it challenges them to run higher.

The International Skyrunning Federation defines its sport as "running in the mountains above 2,000-meter (6,562 feet) altitude where the climbing difficulty does not exceed II° grade and the **incline** is over 30 percent."

In Extreme Skyrunning races, there are often no trails, and the athlete's balance and footing are tested along with stamina.

The sport was founded in 1992 by Marino Giacometti and has grown in popularity ever since. The federation estimates that there are about 50,000 skyrunners in the world from 65 countries and **sanctions** about 200 separate races each year.

The ISF's most popular series is the Skyrunner World Series, which includes three to eight events in four separate categories held around the world from the United States to Malaysia. The categories are Sky, Ultra, Vertical, and Extreme, with races ranging from three in the Extreme category to eight in Sky. Aside from the World Cup series, the ISF also hosts a World Championships in each category annually.

In Sky, races are less than 50 km (31 miles). In Ultra, races are longer than 50 km (31 miles). In Vertical, the race is run uphill with a minimum incline of 25 percent. In the Extreme category, races are run on courses where there are often no trails to follow, only markings, and include super-technical **ridge** running.

Dealing with uneven terrain is part of the challenge in skyrunning.

Sidebar

Kílian Jornet Burgada is a Spaniard who has won six overall Skyrunner World Series Championships and 29 individual World Series races. Jornet is one of the world's premier ultramarathoners. In 2008, he set a world record by running 170 km (106 miles) in 20 hours.

His female counterpart is Sweden's Emelie Forsberg, winner of 13 ISF World Series events and four championships. She is also the 2014 ISF world champion in the Ultra category.

Text-Dependent Questions

1. What is the minimum altitude for a skyrunning race?
2. Approximately how many skyrunners are there in the world?
3. What is the minimum incline for a Vertical skyrunning race?

Research Project

Go for a run around your neighborhood, and measure and record your heart rate, distance, and speed. At another time, travel to a place with higher elevation, and do the same run. Note the differences in your results.

Educational Video

Scan here to see skyrunning in action!

Want to Participate?

Check out some of these incredible places to either participate or watch these amazing mountain sports around the world.

Free Climbing:

Red River Gorge, Slade, KY

Discover world-class rock climbing with more than 1,600 routes of wide-ranging difficulty.

Here are more great places to free climb:

Acadia National Park, Mt. Desert, ME

Spectacular granite walls rise out of the Atlantic Ocean at this home to some classic seaside routes.

Yosemite National Park, Yosemite Valley, CA

Home to the famed El Capitan, this place of legends also has routes accessible to climbers of all skill levels.

Red River Gorge, Slade, KY

Ouray, CO

Ice Climbing

Cascade Waterfall, Banff, Alberta, Canada
The WI3-rated climb is a Banff area classic. It is about 1,000 (305 m) feet high.

Here are more great places to ice climb:
Ouray, CO
Here in the "Switzerland of America" there are more than 200 climbs available December through March.

Rjukan, Norway
Northern Europe's top site has six distinct climbing areas. The winter is harsh, so February and March are prime climbing months.

Bouldering:

Joe's Valley, UT

Hillsides lined with sandstone rock make this valley a bouldering paradise. The rocks are perfect, and the scenery is spectacular.

Here are some more places to climb boulders:

Bishop, CA

Located on the eastern slope of the Sierra Nevadas, Bishop is strewn with both volcanic and granite boulders that present excellent problems for climbers to solve.

Fontainebleau, France

Thousands of problems await here. Late autumn is the best time for climbing on sandstone boulders of every grade level.

Bishop, CA

Canyoneering:

Arenal Volcano, Costa Rica
Amazing rock faces, cascading waterfalls, lush rainforest—what more could a canyoneer ask for? The region has great family-friendly routes as well.

Find other amazing canyons to explore:
Agawa Canyon, Canada
Just outside the capital city of Ottawa, this protected wilderness area is accessible only by train. After that, it's all legwork through the natural splendors of the canyon.

Arenal Volcano, Costa Rica

Zion National Park, UT
Shallow streams surrounded by towering canyon walls and steep gorges begging to be rappelled into are just two of the pleasures that can be found at this Utah treasure.

Solo climbing:

Grand Teton National Park, Jackson, WY
These mountains are known as the "American Alps" for good reason. This might be the best solo climbing spot in the continental United States.

Here are other great places to solo climb:
Fair Head, Northern Ireland
The UK is one of the most geologically diverse areas in the world. Fair Head is home to the famous Complete Scream, a 70-m (300 foot) dolerite rock face.

Red Rock Canyon, NV

Red Rock Canyon, NV
Multi-pitch climbing is the name of the game in this rugged desert landscape outside Las Vegas.

Further Reading:

Doeden, Matt. *Can You Survuve Extreme Mountain Climbing? (You Choose: Survival).* North Mankato, MN: Capstone Press, 2014.

MacDonald, Dougald. *Accidents in North American Mountaineering.* Golden, CO: American Alpine Club. 2015.

Miske, Charles. *Elbrus Race 2013 (Seven Summits Quest).* Create Space Independent Publishing. 2013.

Internet Resources:

International Skyrunning Federation
http://www.skyrunning.com/

International Federation of Sports Climbing
http://www.ifsc-climbing.org/

International Climbing and Mountaineering Federation
http://www.theuiaa.org/

Commission Internationale de Canyon
http://www.cic-canyoning.org/index-en.php

Photo Credits:

Cover: hektoR/Shutterstock.com, Ammit Jack/Shutterstock.com, Artem Novichenko/Shutterstock.com, Roberto Caucino/Shutterstock.com; Page 3: Paulo Resende/Dreamstime.com; Page 6: Philcold/Dreamstime.com; Page 7: Hugoht/Dreamstime.com; Page 8: Pancaketom/Dreamstime.com; Page 9: Bhairav/Dreamstime.com; Page 10: Galyna Andrushko/Dreamstime.com; Page 11: Anton Petrus/Dreamstime.com, Yanlev/Dreamstime.com; Page 12: Aprescindere/Dreamstime.com; Page 13: Justforever/Dreamstime.com; Page 14: Matthew Swartz/Dreamstime.com; Page 15: Lawrence Willard/Dreamstime.com, Alexander Zhiltsov/Dreamstime.com; Page 16: Arne9001/Dreamstime.com; Page 17: Nuno4040/Dreamstime.com; Page 18: Mikhail Dudarev/Dreamstime.com; Page 19: Jakub Cejpek/Dreamstime.com, Pancaketom/Dreamstime.com; Page 20: Tyler Olson/Dreamstime.com; Page 21: Aprescindere/Dreamstime.com; Page 22: Pavalache Stelian/Dreamstime.com Page 23: Agency/Dreamstime.com, Nouubon/Dreamstime.com; Page 24: Galina Barskaya/Dreamstime.com; Page 25: Anja Peternelj/Dreamstime.com; Page 26: Jakub Cejpek/Dreamstime.com; Page 27: Roberto Caucino/Dreamstime.com, Jan Vančura/Dreamstime.com; Page 28: Jakub Cejpek/Dreamstime.com; Page 29: Neil Denize/Dreamstime.com; Page 30: Ammit/Dreamstime.com; Page 31: Delstudio/Dreamstime.com, Isabel Poulin/Dreamstime.com; Page 32: Peter Montgomery/Dreamstime.com; Page 33: Oleg Kozlov/Dreamstime.com; Page 34: Karl_kanal/Dreamstime.com; Page 35: Peter Montgomery/Dreamstime.com, Tatiana Oleshkevich/Dreamstime.com; Page 36: Michelangelo Oprandi/Dreamstime.com; Page 37: Michelangelo Oprandi/Dreamstime.com; Page 38: Michelangelo Oprandi/Dreamstime.com; Page 39: Alexander Uhrin/Dreamstime.com, Michelangelo Oprandi/Dreamstime.com; Page 40: Oliclimb/Dreamstime.com; Page 41: Robert Fullerton/Dreamstime.com; Page 42: Tom Grundy/Dreamstime.com; Page 43: Cedric Carter/Dreamstime.com; Page 45: Robert Fullerton/Dreamstime.com; Page 46: Gary Boisvert/Dreamstime.com; Page 47: Edite Artmann/Dreamstime.com

Video Credits:

Free Climbing - http://x-qr.net/1GcU
Aid Climbing - http://x-qr.net/1Ggc
Bouldering - http://x-qr.net/1GxG
Solo Climbing - http://x-qr.net/1H8y
Ice Climbing - http://x-qr.net/1GcD
Canyoneering - http://x-qr.net/1GGm
Mountaineering - http://x-qr.net/1GkY
Skyrunning - http://x-qr.net/1Hbt

Author Bio:

Andrew Luke is a former journalist, reporting on both sports and general news for many years at television stations in various locations across the United States affiliated with NBC, CBS, and Fox. Prior to his journalism career, he worked with the Boston Red Sox Major League baseball team. An avid writer and sports enthusiast, he has authored 11 other books on sports topics. In his downtime Andrew enjoys family time with his wife and two young children and attending hockey and baseball games in his home city of Pittsburgh, PA.

Index:

In this index, page numbers in bold italic font indicate photos or videos.